W9-AFS-647

Published by Raintree Steck-Vaughn Publishers, an imprint of Steck-Vaughn Company.

Library of Congress Cataloging-in-Publication Data
　　Mesopotamia/by Tami Deedrick.
　　　　p.cm.—(Ancient civilizations)
　　Includes bibliographical references and index.
　　ISBN 0-7398-3584-X
　　　　1. Iraq—Civilization—To 634—Juvenile literature. [1. Iraq—Civilization—To 634.] I. Title. II. Ancient civilizations (Raintree Steck-Vaughn)
DS71 .D43 2001
935—dc21

　　　　　　　　　　　　　　　　　　　　　　　　　　　　　　2001019860

Printed and bound in the United States of America
1 2 3 4 5 6 7 8 9 10 WZ 05 04 03 02 01

Produced by Compass Books

Photo Acknowledgments
Corbis/Roger Wood, cover; Dean Conger, title page; Gianni Dagli Orti, 6, 10, 14, 16, 19, 20, 25,
　　26, 29, 32, 36; David Lees, 9; Charles Lenars, 22; Bettmann, 30;
　　Diego Lezama Orezzoli, 34; Francoise de Mulder, 43

Content Consultants
Christopher Rose
Outreach Coordinator
Center for Middle Eastern Studies
The University of Texas at Austin

Don L. Curry
Educational Author, Editor, Consultant, and Columnist